MACHINES, CARS, BOATS, AND AIRPLANES

Alan Snow

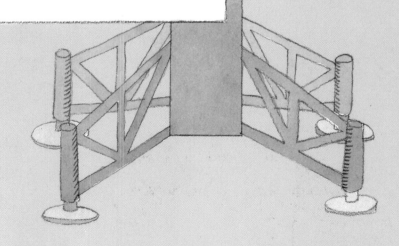

Derrydale Books
New York

On the Farm

There is a special machine for almost every job on the farm, from plowing the fields to milking the cows.

Tractors do most of the work on the farm.

They have powerful engines so they can pull trailers.

And they have big wheels so they can drive across muddy fields.

I'm pulling a plow.

The **plow** breaks up the ground.

*I'm pulling a **harrow**.*

The **harrow** breaks up the ground even more.

I'm pulling a seed drill.

The **seed drill** sows the seeds.

Now the wheat is ready to cut.

The **combine harvester** cuts the wheat and separates it into stalk and grain. The grain is dried. The stalks, called straw, are used as feed. ▶

combine harvester

grain

tractor

trailer

wheat

The grain is made into flour.

flour   flour   bread rolls   cakes   cereal

In the Forest

Wood comes from trees. We use wood for many things. We use logs to make a warm fire, planks of cut trees to build a home, and wood pulp to make paper. How many things can you think of that are made of wood?

A towline is used to haul logs out of hilly forests on a steel cable. ▶

Baby trees are planted in nurseries to stop animals from eating them. ▼▼

When the trees are big enough they are cut down with **chainsaws**.
◀

Special **tractors** drag or carry the logs out of the forest. ▲

Buzz, buzz!

*I'm trimming off the **branches**.*

hydraulic grab

I'm loading the logs onto my truck to take them to the mill.

*I'm cutting the tree into **logs**.*

Wood is used to make paper.

Logs are taken to the paper mill.

They are shredded and mixed with water to make pulp.

paper-making machine

The pulp is spread out, dried, and pressed to make paper.

Paper is used to make newspapers, books, and magazines.

In the Mine

Miners use a lot of machines to help them tunnel underground and dig out minerals and metals like salt, coal, or gold. Here is a picture of a coal mine.

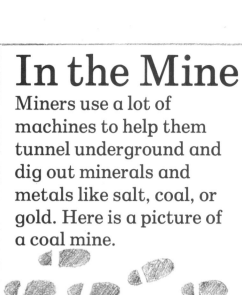

gold   jewels

tin   coal

salt   steel

Inside this tower there is an engine which runs the elevator up and down the shaft.

Here are some things which are made from materials dug out of mines.

train
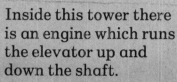

air

Big **cutting machines** dig the coal out of the coal face.
▼

shaft

tunnel

Holes are drilled in the **coal face** to put explosives in.
▼

Time for lunch!

coal

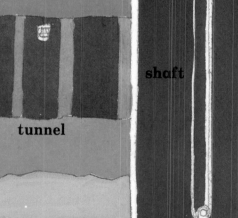

Explosives are used to break up the coal.
▼

The **coal train** carries coal to the shaft.
▲

Hydraulic props hold up the roof.
▼

The **cage** carries miners to work and lifts coal out of the mine.

The explosives are set off using a **detonator**.
▼

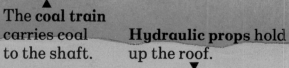

On the Road

Many big machines are used when making roads. Each machine has a specific job to do.

This is how a road is built. First a surveyor plans the best way for the road to go. Then an engineer works out how to build it. Then the workmen set the machines to work!
▼

Roads need to be flat. A **scraper** removes the bumps, levelling the earth.

A **bulldozer** pushes any rocks out of the way.

Dump trucks carry the rocks and soil away.

A **grader** smoothes the earth.

A **paving machine** lays down the asphalt.

A **roller** smooths the surface to make it flat.

Four-wheel drive vehicle

exhaust

shovel

scoop

surveyor

A **back hoe** like this one is used for all kinds of jobs. It has a bucket in front and a shovel at the back for digging holes. It has a very powerful engine.

Asphalt, a mixture of stones and tar, forms the smooth surface on top of the road.

Together, many workers build houses. It is hard work that makes you hungry. Here is how one kind of house is built.

Roofers nail tiles to the rafters to keep out the rain.
▼

A **bricklayer** builds the walls on top of a concrete base called a foundation.
▼

▲
Carpenters put in the doors, floors, and windows and put up the roof rafters.

▲
Painters paint the walls and woodwork.

▲
Electricians put in the wires and switches.

▲
Plumbers put in the water pipes and faucets.

The mortar which holds the bricks together is made from a mixture of sand, cement, and water.

cement

sand

wheelbarrow

cement mixer

On the Railroad

All trains run on rails, but not all trains are the same. Some carry people while some carry heavy loads like wood, coal, or milk. Here are some different sights you could see near a railroad.

signal box

Signals are like traffic lights. They are worked by a **signal person** who directs the train traffic.

overhead wire

This is an **electric train**. It has an electric motor which turns the wheels. The electricity comes from overhead wires.

Hoppers carry loads like sand. A door opens at the bottom which empties the load from the hopper.

Rail tanks carry liquid loads, like milk or gas.

coal car

The **driver** sits in the **cab**.

All aboard!

passenger car

rail

The **guard** tells the driver when it's time to go.

The Service Station

Service stations are places where mechanics repair cars. Some service stations also sell fuel which cars and trucks need to make them run.

Body Shop

Scratched or dented cars need to be repainted. Dents are knocked out and new paint is sprayed on with a **spray-gun**. Car paint is poisonous, so the painter must wear a mask.

Exhaust fans keep the air clean.

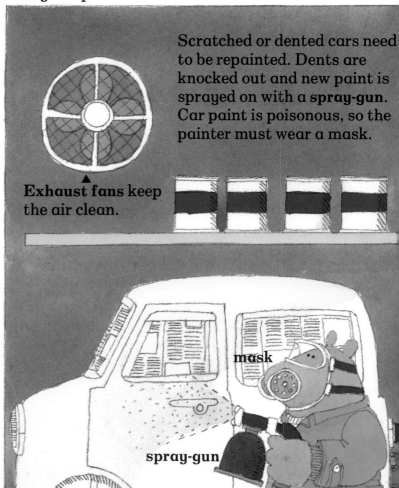

mask

spray-gun

air hose

Salesroom

This is where new cars are sold. There are many different types of cars. Some are big, some small, some very fast. There are 411 million cars and trucks in the world. That's a lot of machines!

The display on the pump shows how much gas you have bought, and how much it costs.

sales person

new car

0000
38.5

gas pump

Repair Shop

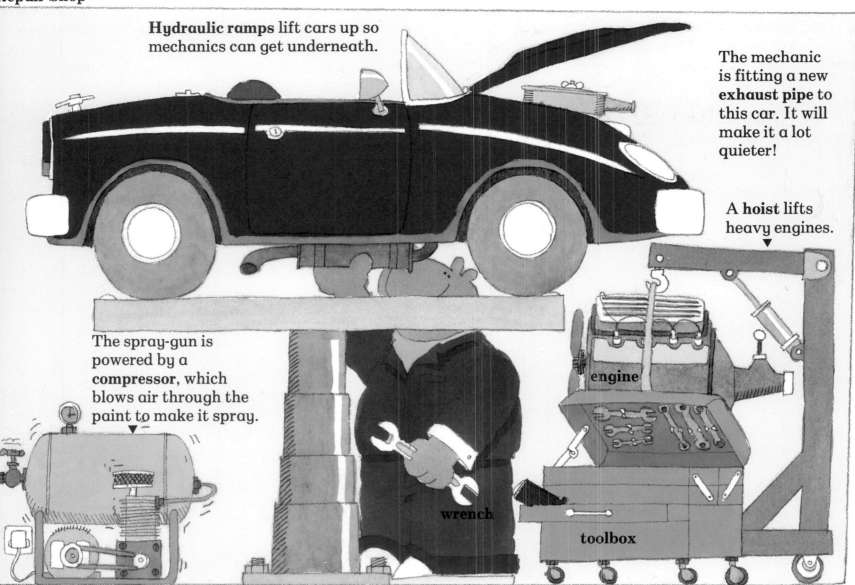

Hydraulic ramps lift cars up so mechanics can get underneath.

The mechanic is fitting a new **exhaust pipe** to this car. It will make it a lot quieter!

A **hoist** lifts heavy engines.

The spray-gun is powered by a **compressor**, which blows air through the paint to make it spray.

engine

wrench

toolbox

Gas Station

All machines need fuel to make them go. Most cars use gasoline as a fuel. The fuel tank in the car is filled from a pump, which pumps gas up from a huge tank underground.

cashier

motorist

What's this do?

valve

flat tire

tire

In the Harbor

Cars are used to move on land, but to travel on water you need a boat. Boats are kept in harbors. Here, they can be loaded and repaired, or just given a new coat of paint.

harbor-master's office

row boat

outboard motor

sail

mast

Inflatable boats are blown full of air to make them float.

Sailboats are blown along by the wind. Some have engines in case the wind stops blowing. ►

I do love to be by the seashore!

funnel

This boat is a **fishing boat**. Its job is to catch fish, crabs, and lobsters.
▼

wheelhouse

winch

bow

hatch

hull

deck

fishing nets

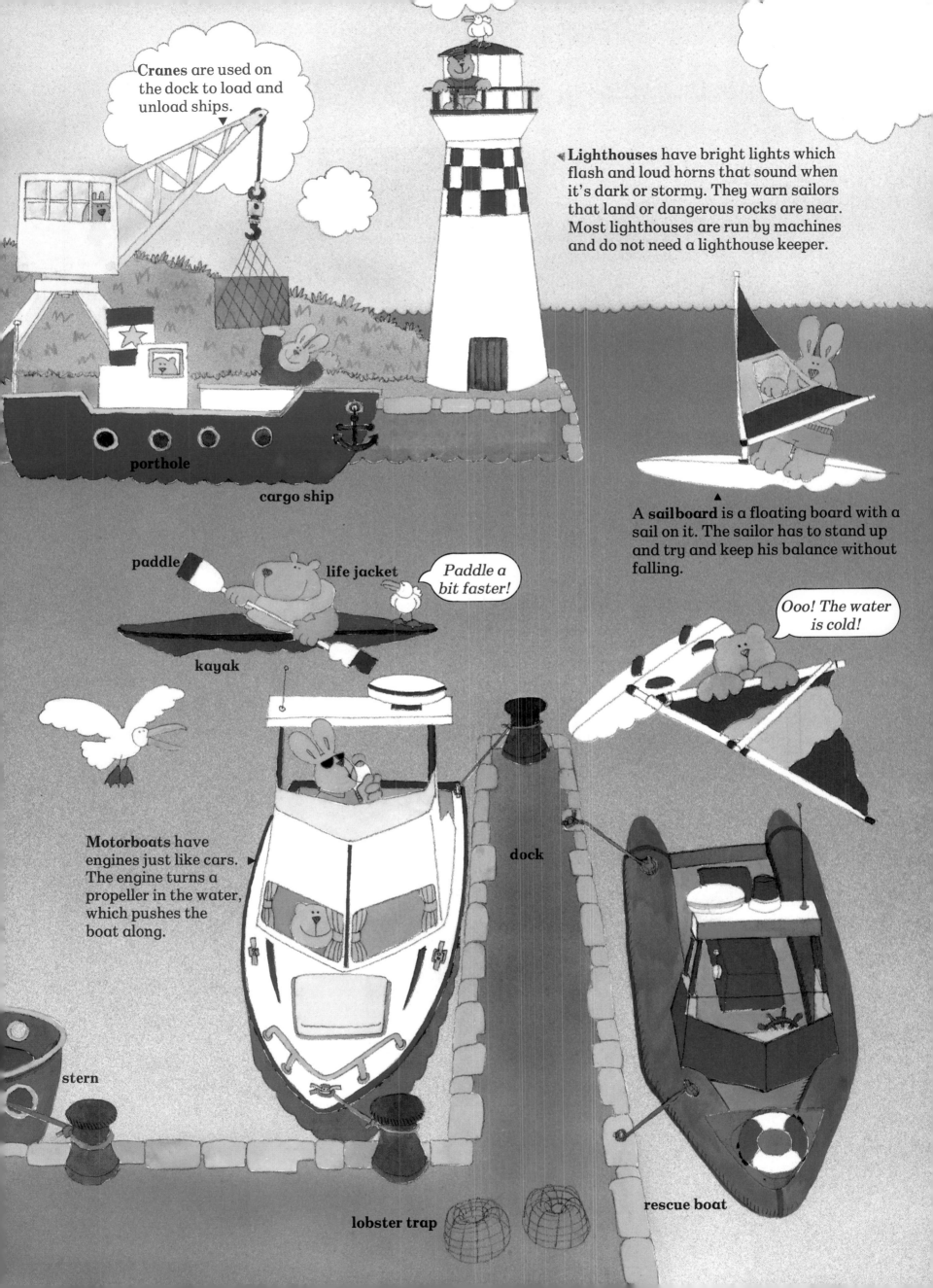

At the Airport

Airports are very busy places. Airplanes and helicopters land and takeoff here every few minutes, and people and their baggage get on and off. Machines of all kinds help the airport run smoothly and safely.

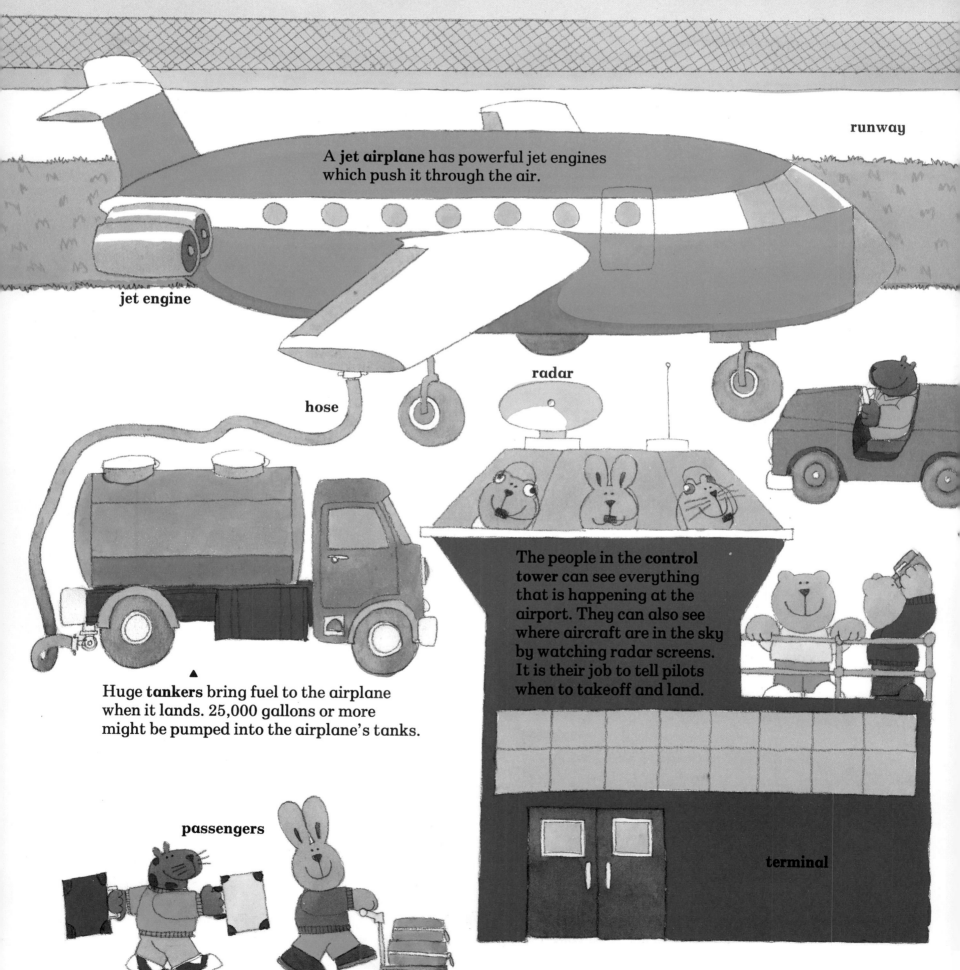

runway

A **jet airplane** has powerful jet engines which push it through the air.

jet engine

hose

radar

The people in the **control tower** can see everything that is happening at the airport. They can also see where aircraft are in the sky by watching radar screens. It is their job to tell pilots when to takeoff and land.

Huge **tankers** bring fuel to the airplane when it lands. 25,000 gallons or more might be pumped into the airplane's tanks.

passengers

terminal

rotor blades

◀ **Helicopters** don't need wings to fly. The big rotor arms on the top lift them up into the air. They can go forward, backward, or stay still and hover.

Put me down!

▲ **Hangars** are big buildings in which airplanes can be kept when they need checking or repairing.

▲ Helicopters can lift people or things up and down like a flying crane.

Airliners are high off the ground. Special steps are wheeled to ◀ the doors so that passengers can get on board.

steps

Some airplanes have a propeller which drives ◀ them through the air. The first airplanes were propeller driven.

wing

propeller

cockpit

tail

tow truck

fuselage

wheels

Before you board an airplane.

Your ticket is checked and your luggage is weighed.

An **x-ray machine** reveals what is inside your luggage.

A **metal detector** checks you!

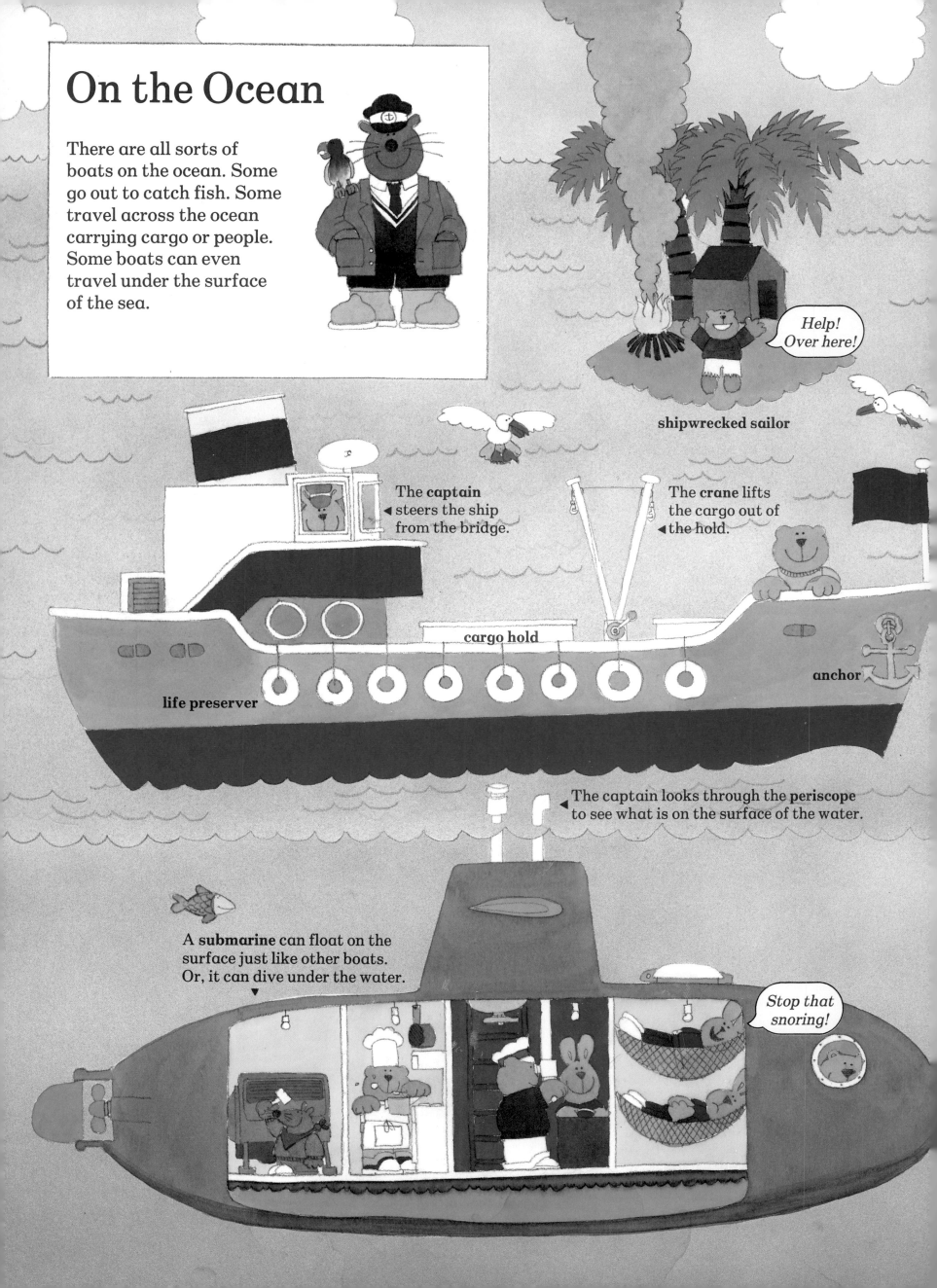

On the Ocean

There are all sorts of boats on the ocean. Some go out to catch fish. Some travel across the ocean carrying cargo or people. Some boats can even travel under the surface of the sea.

Help! Over here!

shipwrecked sailor

The **captain** steers the ship from the bridge.

The **crane** lifts the cargo out of the hold.

cargo hold

anchor

life preserver

The captain looks through the **periscope** to see what is on the surface of the water.

A **submarine** can float on the surface just like other boats. Or, it can dive under the water.

Stop that snoring!

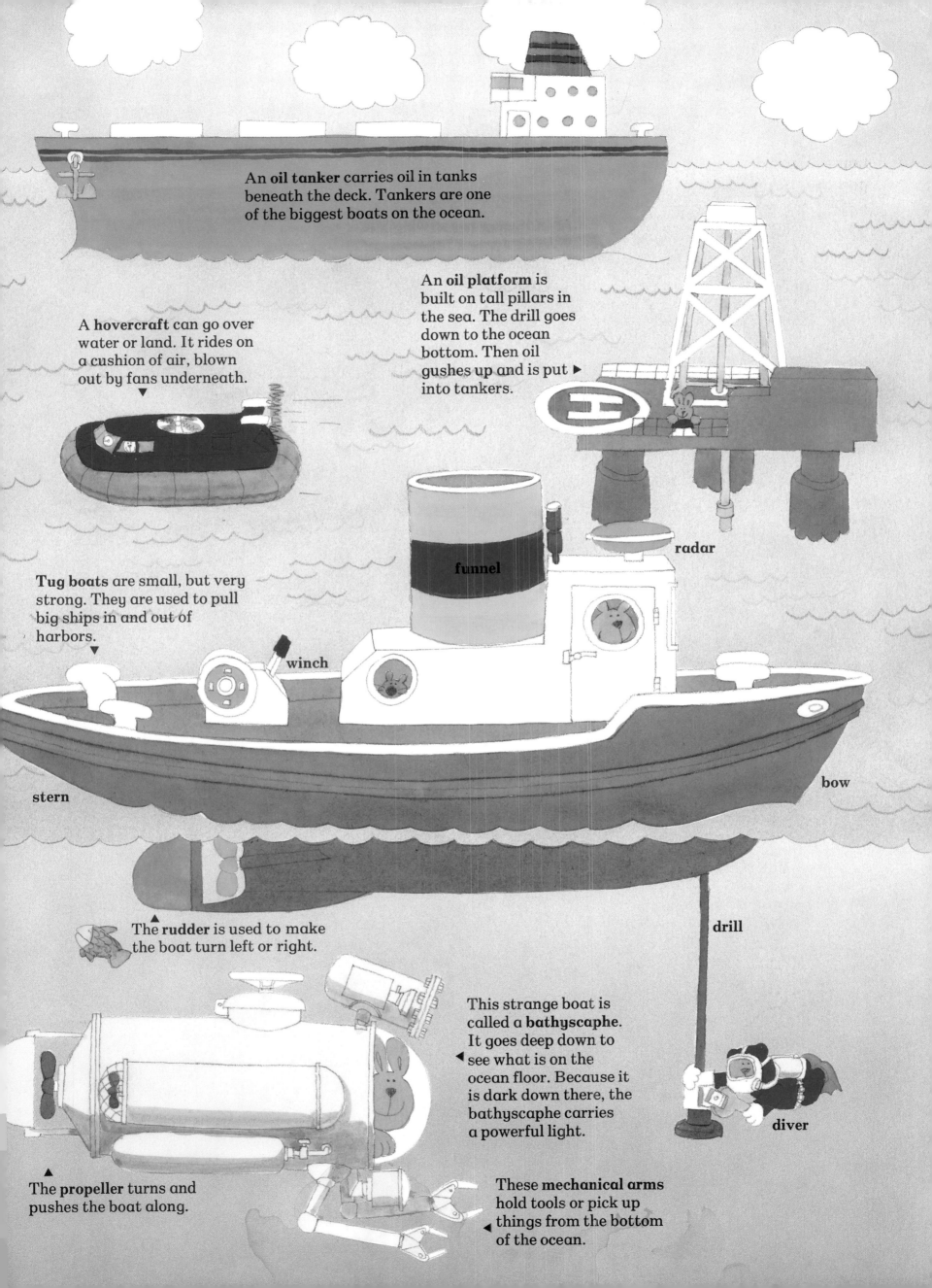

An **oil tanker** carries oil in tanks beneath the deck. Tankers are one of the biggest boats on the ocean.

A **hovercraft** can go over water or land. It rides on a cushion of air, blown out by fans underneath. ▼

An **oil platform** is built on tall pillars in the sea. The drill goes down to the ocean bottom. Then oil gushes up and is put ▶ into tankers.

radar

Tug boats are small, but very strong. They are used to pull big ships in and out of harbors. ▼

funnel

winch

stern

bow

drill

▲ The **rudder** is used to make the boat turn left or right.

This strange boat is called a **bathyscaphe**. It goes deep down to ◀ see what is on the ocean floor. Because it is dark down there, the bathyscaphe carries a powerful light.

diver

▲ The **propeller** turns and pushes the boat along.

These **mechanical arms** hold tools or pick up ◀ things from the bottom of the ocean.

At Home

There are a lot of machines in your own home. Most of them are powered by electricity. How many machines do you have in your home?